THE AGE OF EMPIRE

British History

THE AGE OF EMPIRE

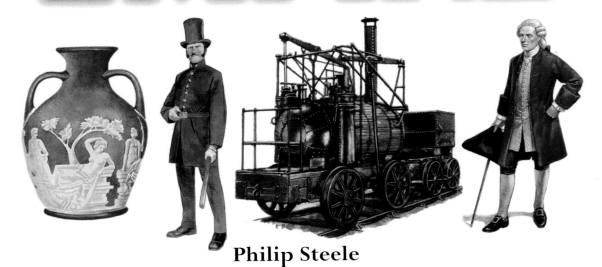

Philip Steele

Miles Kelly
PUBLISHING

First published in 2002 by Miles Kelly Publishing Ltd,
Bardfield Centre, Great Bardfield, Essex, CM7 4SL

ISBN 1-84236-144-9

2 4 6 8 10 9 7 5 3 1

Some material in this book can also be found
in the *Encyclopedia of British History*
Project Manager: Kate Miles
Art Director: Clare Sleven
Artwork Commissioning: Janice Bracken & Lesley Cartlidge
Picture Research: Ruth Boardman
Referencing: Liberty Newton
Assistant: Lisa Clayden
Repro: DPI

Contact us by email: info@mileskelly.net
Website: www.mileskelly.net

Printed in Hong Kong

CONTENTS

INTRODUCTION

Small and surrounded by the ocean, the British Isles seemed unlikely to become a great world power. However the English Channel protected the islands from invading armies and its seafarers were in a good position to profit from trade with North America, Africa and Asia.

In the 1700s, Britain came under the rule of kings from Hanover, in Germany. The British army put down rebellions in Scotland and also in Ireland, which joined the United Kingdom in 1801.

Captain James Cook (1728-1799) was an English naval officer who led expeditions to the New World. He was killed in a skirmish on the island of Hawaii.

Britain engaged in long wars with other nations in Europe. These conflicts soon extended around the globe. France, Britain's great rival, was defeated in India and Canada. In the 1770s Britain lost its precious colonies in eastern North America, as a result of the American War of Independence.

Despite this setback, during the long reign of Queen Victoria after 1837, Britain's overseas empire became the greatest the world had ever seen. It now extended over large areas of Africa, Asia, Australia and the Pacific islands.

Prince Charles Edward Stuart (1720-1788) was known to the Scots as Bonnie Prince Charlie and to the English as the Young Pretender.

Richard Trevithick (1771-1833) was a British engineer who built a steam road locomotive in 1801 and the first steam engine to run on rails in 1804.

Factories in huge new cities manufactured goods which could be sold around the world. Power and wealth for the ruling classes were achieved at great cost, both at home and abroad. Poor working conditions, poverty and sickness were widespread. Famine killed thousands in Ireland. Workers called for political reform, the right to vote, the right to form trade unions, the right to a decent wage and a healthy life. It was a long hard battle, but conditions did slowly get better.

Queen Victoria's death in 1901 marked the end of an age. The century that would followed brought new conflicts on a global scale, a decline of British political and industrial power and rifts within the Union. However it also brought a fairer sharing out of wealth and social justice, and votes for women. The lives we lead in Britain and Ireland, the shape of our cities and the rich variety of ethnic groups who live in them today, are all still rooted in the history of the 1700s and 1800s, the age of industry and empire.

The key to Britain's success lay in its technology. Britain was itself rich in resources such as coal. It became the first industrial power in the world and the first to develop railways. Britiain could also profit from the minerals and crops of its growing empire.

Isambard Kingdom Brunel (1806-1859) designed the SS Great Eastern which laid the first transatlantic telegraph cable in 1857.

A WORLD POWER

1714–1901

THE WORLD AT A GLANCE

ELSEWHERE IN EUROPE

1720
Russia defeats Sweden in the Great Northern War, gains Estonia

1740
Frederick II ('the Great') becomes King of Prussia, Maria Theresa becomes Empress of Austria

1789
Outbreak of the French Revolution in Paris. King Louis XVI is executed in 1793

1804
Napoleon Bonaparte is crowned Emperor of France. Draws up new code of laws

1815
The Congress of Vienna redraws the map of Europe. Poland is united with Russia

1821
Greeks rise against Turkish rule. Greece is recognized as independent in 1832

1871
Germany unites as a single empire under the rule of Wilhelm I, King of Prussia

1871
Rome becomes capital of a united Italy for the first time since the Roman empire

ASIA

1739
Persia (Iran) invades India and captures the city of Delhi

1750
The French gain control of southern India

1819
British empire-builder Stamford Raffles founds modern port at Singapore

1858
Rule of India passes from the East India Company to the British government

1867
The Meiji Restoration: Japan modernizes under the rule of emperor Mutsuhito

1883
One of the world's worst ever volcanic eruptions destroys Krakatoa island

1891
Work begins on the Trans-Siberian Railway (from Moscow to the Pacific)

1900
Defeat of nationalists ('Boxers') rebelling against foreign influence in China

AFRICA

1720
Sultan of Zanzibar takes control of the East African coast

1730
Revival of the Bornu empire, south of the Sahara desert

1806
Britain gains control of Cape Colony, South Africa, from the Dutch

1818
Shaka founds the Zulu kingdom in South Africa

1822
Liberia is founded in West Africa, as a colony for liberated slaves

1869
Suez Canal opens, European powers have growing influence in Egypt

1896
Emperor Menelik II of Ethiopia defeats an Italian army at Adowa

1899
Boer War begins between British and Afrikaners in South Africa

"A British empire is founded on cotton, coal and toil…"

the Portland Vase

NORTH AMERICA

1718
French found the port of New Orleans, Louisiana

1759
Britain defeats France to capture the Canadian city of Quebec

1776
American colonists declare their independence from Britain

1823
Mexico becomes an independent republic

1838
Slavery ended in Jamaica and other British Caribbean colonies

1861
Civil war in the United States (until 1865, abolition of slavery)

1867
Canada becomes a self-governing Dominion within British empire

1876
Native Americans defeat US Cavalry at the Battle of Little Bighorn

SOUTH AMERICA

1763
Rio de Janeiro becomes capital of Spanish Brazil

1780
Uprising of indigenous peoples in Peru under Tupac Amaru II

1816
Argentina declares its independence from Spain

1818
Chile becomes independent from Spain, under Bernardo O'Higgins

1819
New Granada (Colombia, Venezuela, Ecuador) independent under Simon Bolívar

1822
Brazil proclaims its independence from Spain under Pedro I

1826
Peru gains its independence from Spain

1888
Slavery is finally abolished in Brazil

OCEANIA

1768
British navigator James Cook visits Tahiti, New Zealand and Australia (to 1771)

1788
British convicts and settlers arrive at Botany Bay, southeast Australia

1840
Treaty of Waitangi: Maori chiefs cede New Zealand to British

1843
First Maori War, start of many conflicts with the British colonists (into the 1860s)

1850
Self-government granted to Britain's Australian colonies (New Zealand 1856)

1851
A Gold Rush begins in Australia

1884
Northeastern New Guinea taken over by Germany. Britain claims the southeast

1901
Australian colonies unite within a federal Commonwealth

10

〜 **1694**
The Bank of England is founded in London

〜 **1715**
The Riot Act is passed, controlling public order

〜 **1720**
The 'South Sea Bubble': financial crash

〜 **1721**
Robert Walpole is first British Prime Minister

〜 **1731**
No 10 Downing Street is residence of Prime Minister

MONEY AND POLITICS

T HE gap between rich and poor people in the British Isles was growing ever wider. London society in the 1730s and 40s is shown up in the paintings and engravings of William Hogarth. Poor families brawl, desperate young mothers drink cheap gin on the street until they fall into a stupor. Adventurers are on the make, climbing their way up the all too corrupt social scale, only to fall back down and end their days in a debtors' prison.

Dealers in shares, or stockjobbers, drove up the trading price far beyond the real value.

The 'South Sea Bubble' crash provided a wealth of material for the newspapers of the day and for political cartoonists.

BANKS AND MONEY

Paper bank notes were first issued in Britain in 1695. There was a growing view of wealth as an abstract idea, of deals made on paper rather than as chests full of gold coins. New companies, many of them founded in order to make money in distant colonies overseas, issued shares. At first these were bought and sold in coffee shops. A Stock Exchange was founded in the City of London in 1773.

THE SOUTH SEA BUBBLE

Trading shares in the hope of making a profit is called speculation. It is a form of gambling, and can lead to reward or ruin. Britain's first great financial crash happened in 1720. Shares in the South Sea Company, founded in 1711 to trade with South America, rose to a ridiculous value, driven up by feverish speculation and crooked government dealings. When this South Sea 'bubble' burst, thousands of people were ruined. Many committed suicide.

PRIME MINISTERS AT NO 10

Because George I spoke no English and was often away in Hanover, government affairs began to be dealt with by his chief ('prime') minister, who chose a working committee of ministers (the 'cabinet'). From 1721 the first – unofficial – Prime Minister was a formidable Whig politician, Sir Robert Walpole. The use of Number 10 Downing Street as the London residence of British Prime Ministers dates back to 1731.

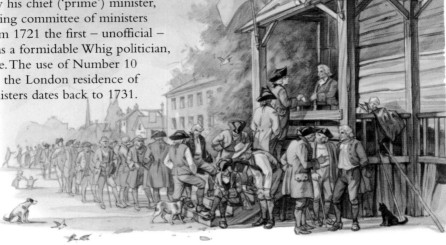

The few men who were allowed to vote did so in public. There was opportunity for bullying and corruption. Drunken crowds, in the pay of one party or another, often rioted at election time.

THE GREAT DEBATERS

Powerful debaters could be heard in the House of Commons. William Pitt the Elder entered politics in 1735, part of a group within the Whigs who were opposed to Walpole. He was a great supporter of Britain's overseas wars. His popular son, William Pitt the Younger, served over 17 years as Prime Minister. His great opponent was Charles Fox, who became a Member of Parliament at the age of just 19.

PRIME MINISTERS OF GREAT BRITAIN

✦ Sir Robert Walpole (Whig)	1721–1742
✦ Earl of Wilmington (Whig)	1742–1743
✦ Henry Pelham (Whig)	1743–1754
✦ Duke of Newcastle (Whig)	1754–1756
✦ Duke of Devonshire (Whig)	1756–1757
✦ Duke of Newcastle (Whig)	1757–1762
✦ Earl of Bute (Tory)	1762–1763
✦ George Grenville (Whig)	1763–1765
✦ Marquess of Rockingham (Whig)	1782
✦ Earl of Shelburne (Whig)	1782–1783
✦ Duke of Portland (coalition)	1783
✦ William Pitt the Younger (Tory)	1783–1801

Robert Walpole entered politics in the reign of Queen Anne and was made Chancellor of the Exchequer by George I, in 1715. He died in 1745.

WHO GETS TO VOTE?

New industries were growing fast. To make a profit, they needed a large workforce but low wages. Economic forces were driving politics along, but the workforce was not represented in Parliament at all. Only a few men with land and money had the vote. In 1789 a revolution broke out in France. British politicians eyed the dramatic events in mainland Europe nervously. Could they happen here?

12

᠖ 1746
French capture Madras, British
base in India

᠖ 1750
British capture Arcot, gain
control of southern India

᠖ 1757
Battle of Plassey, Britain gains
Bengal, India

᠖ 1759
Britain captures Quebec,
Canada, from France

᠖ 1763
Treaty of Paris, Britain gains
Canada and Caribbean islands

'BROWN BESS'

To fire a musket, the cock first had to be set at the safety position. The metal pan was opened, filled with a small amount of gunpowder and closed. The main charge of gunpowder and a ball were then rammed down the muzzle. When the trigger was pressed, it released a hammer containing a flint. This struck against the raised pan cover, dropping sparks into the gunpowder. When this ignited, the shot was fired.

Ramrod
Each new charge had to be rammed down the muzzle. The iron ramrod could be fitted under the barrel.

Long barrel
The great length of the musket's barrel was meant to help it fire straight, but it was not very efficient. Later gun barrels were 'rifled', having spiral grooves that made the bullet spin.

Bayonet
A long dagger could be fitted to the barrel for hand-to-hand fighting.

The flintlock
The flintlock mechanism was slow to use and unreliable. Gunpowder had to be kept dry.

British troops carried a type of flintlock musket known as 'Brown Bess'.

FARAWAY LANDS

B Y THE 1740s, Europe's most powerful countries were warring with each other around the world. The stakes were high – rich trade and new lands. The first overseas colonies were often founded by commercial companies, which had their own armies and fleets of ships. Local people were powerless in the face of heavily armed European troops.

THE EAST INDIA COMPANY

As India's mighty Moghul empire fell into decline in the 1740s and 50s, the British East India Company seized land from local rulers. It ended up controlling much of the country, fighting its French rivals every step of the way. British success was largely due to a brilliant general called Robert Clive. By fair means or foul, Company officials became hugely rich. When they returned to Britain, they found themselves not only envied but mocked for their new-found wealth. They were nicknamed 'nabobs' (from the Hindi word *nawab*, 'governor').

≈≈ 1768
James Cook explores the Pacific Ocean (to 1771)

≈≈ 1770
James Cook claims New South Wales, Australia for Britain

≈≈ 1779
James Cook is killed by Hawaiians

≈≈ 1789
Crew of *HMS Bounty* mutiny on Pacific voyage

13

ACROSS THE ATLANTIC

In Canada, the story was similar. The French had a colony on the St Lawrence River, while the British Hudson's Bay Company controlled land to the north. In 1759 British troops captured Quebec. By the Treaty of Paris, which ended the Seven Years' War in 1763, Britain gained Canada and also some of France's Caribbean islands – Tobago, St Vincent, Grenada, and Dominica.

To capture Quebec in 1759, British troops climbed up cliffs to take the French by surprise. Both commanders – James Wolf and the Marquis de Montcalm – died in the battle.

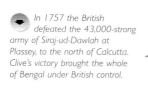

In 1757 the British defeated the 43,000-strong army of Siraj-ud-Dawlah at Plassey, to the north of Calcutta. Clive's victory brought the whole of Bengal under British control.

FROM AFRICA TO ENGLAND

In about 1760 a 10 year-old Nigerian boy called Olaudah Equiano was kidnapped from his West African home and sold to slave traders. He was transported to the Caribbean, but ended up buying his freedom from his master. He became a sailor and took ship to London, where he campaigned against slavery until his death in 1797. He wrote about his experiences in a book published in 1789.

AUSTRALIA AND THE PACIFIC

In 1761, a naval captain called James Cook sailed to explore the Pacific Ocean. He mapped the coast of New Zealand and landed in Australia, claiming New South Wales for Britain. On later voyages, Cook explored the coasts of Antarctica and discovered many Pacific islands. He also sailed along the North America's west coast as far as the Bering Strait. He was killed in Hawaii in 1779.

James Cook was a Yorkshireman, the son of a farm worker. He captained British ships to the far ends of the Earth. A brilliant navigator, he was well liked by his crews.

∞ 1732
Colony of Georgia is founded,
named after George II

∞ 1763
Treaty of Paris gives
Britain territory west
to the Mississippi

∞ 1765
Britain attempts to tax North
American colonists

∞ 1773
'Boston Tea Party':
colonists throw tea
into the harbour

∞ 1774
British close Boston harbour
and send in troops

THE LOSS · OF · AMERICA

B Y 1763, Britain had gained control of North America from the Atlantic shore to the Mississippi River. Their lands were divided into 13 colonies. The colonists were independently minded. Many of them were descended from people who had come to America to escape injustice – Puritans, Quakers, political rebels. They resented the British government's strict controls on shipping and trade across the Atlantic Ocean. They were furious when the British demanded that they pay for the wars against the French – through taxation.

Native American warriors were used by the British in their colonial wars with the French.

In 1776 Britain recruited about 29,000 Hessian troops (German mercenaries) to fight for them in North America.

A colonist militia the Green Mountain Boys were formed in Vermont as early as 1770.

In 1773 colonists disguised themselves as Native Americans and boarded British ships anchored in Boston harbour. They threw the cargoes of tea into the sea. This protest against taxation was jokingly called the 'Boston Tea Party'.

TAXES – BUT NO VOTES

Britain first attempted to tax its American colonies in 1765. A costly tax was placed on all legal documents. This was soon withdrawn, but it was replaced by other taxes. Customs duties had to be paid on European goods. The colonists declared that it was unfair for them to pay taxes to a government in which they were not represented. Britain responded by sending in troops and in 1770 they massacred protestors in Boston.

The prosperous port of Charles Town or Charleston, in South Carolina, had been founded in 1670. Its inhabitants included people of English, Irish, Scottish, Dutch, German, French and African descent.

🌀 1775	🌀 1776	🌀 1778	🌀 1781	🌀 1812	15
War of Independence: colonists raise army under Washington	Declaration of Independence by the colonists	John Paul Jones raids the Scottish coast	Britain defeated at Yorktown	War between Britain and the USA (until 1814)	

AN AMERICAN REVOLUTION

The American War of Independence broke out in April 1775 when George Washington defeated the British at Lexington. In 1776 the American colonists declared their independence from Britain. One of them, a Scot called John Paul Jones, sailed across the Atlantic to attack British shipping. In 1778 both France and the Netherlands joined the American side against Britain. The fighting continued until 1781, when the British surrendered at Yorktown, in Virginia. Britain had lost its richest prize.

BATTLES IN AMERICA
American War of Independence

♣ Bunker Hill	1775
British victory	
♣ Lexington	1775
American victory	
♣ Saratoga Springs	1777
American victory	
♣ Brandywine Creek	1777
British victory	
♣ Yorktown	1781
American victory	

THE RIGHTS OF MAN

Thomas Paine was an English political thinker. He went to live in Philadelphia in 1774 and became a keen supporter of American independence. In England in 1791, he started to write *The Rights of Man*, supporting the French Revolution and calling for an end to monarchy in Britain. Accused of treason, Paine fled to France. His last years were spent in America, but his refusal to believe in God made him few friends in his old age.

THE WAR OF 1812

In 1783 Britain finally recognised the United States of America as an independent country. However in 1812, when Britain was at war with France, it tried to prevent the free movement of American shipping. War broke out again. In 1814 British troops occupied Washington and burned down government buildings. Peace was made, but before news of it reached America, General Andrew Jackson defeated the British at New Orleans. Within a hundred years, the USA would have become the world's most powerful nation.

1709
Abraham Darby uses
coke instead of charcoal
to smelt iron

1712
Thomas Newcomen's piston-
operated steam engine

1730
Charles Townshend's
theories on the rotation
of crops

1733
John Kay's flying shuttle for
the weaving industry

1733
Jethro Tull publishes farming
guide: *Horse-Hoeing Husbandry*

ΠEW TECHΠOLOGIES

BRITAIN was rich in coal and its overseas empire could provide valuable raw materials such as cotton or jute. These new lands also offered a huge market for manufactured goods such as textiles. Clever inventions made it possible to produce goods more quickly and cheaply than ever before. A new system of canals made it much easier to move goods from cities to ports. An 'industrial revolution' had begun.

Tin and copper had been mined in Cornwall since ancient times. By 1800 this industry was being transformed, with steam engines pumping out the mines, and with new roads and foundries being constructed. Soon the Cornish mines were employing 50,000 workers.

MILLS AND MINES

Britain became the world's first industrial country. By 1757 glowing furnaces rose from the heads of the South Wales valleys. The great ironworks at Carron brought industry to the Scottish Lowlands in 1759. The world's first iron bridge spanned the River Severn in Shropshire, England, by 1779. Factories and mills spread through Yorkshire, Lancashire, the English Midlands. Tin was mined in Cornwall, lead in Derbyshire, copper in Wales. The poet William Blake wrote of 'dark, satanic mills' appearing in a 'green and pleasant land'.

From the 1760s, a network of canals was dug by gangs of labourers called navigators, or 'navvies'. Pottery and other manufactured goods were transported in horse-drawn boats.

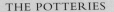

∽ 1742
Cotton factories in Birmingham
and Northampton

∽ 1759
Worsley to Manchester
canal. By 1772 it reached
the River Mersey

∽ 1769
Josiah Wedgwood founds
Etruria pottery works near
Hanley

∽ 1774
James Watt's steam engine is
manufactured

∽ 1779
Samuel Crompton's 'spinning
mule' for textile mills

17

STEAM AND COAL

Steam power was developed in
1712 by two Devonshire
engineers, Thomas Savery and
Thomas Newcomen, to pump
out water from mines. In the
1770s the steam engine was
perfected by a Scottish
engineering genius called
James Watt. His successful
steam pumps allowed deep
mine shafts to be bored into
the Northumberland and
Durham coalfields.

*Massive, hissing steam
engines provided the power
for Britain's industrial revolution.*

*The spinning-jenny of 1768
was a machine which
operated several spindles at once.
It was developed in Lancashire,
England, by James Hargreaves and
mechanic Thomas Higgs, who
named it after his daughter.*

A TEXTILE REVOLUTION

Few industries changed so much in the 1750s and 60s as
spinning and weaving. Output soared as new spinning frames
and shuttles were invented by pioneers such as Richard
Arkwright, James Hargreaves and Samuel Crompton. Work once
carried out in the home was transferred to big textile mills
powered by water or, later, by steam. By the 1800s, the
industrial revolution was gaining speed. It would change the
world forever.

THE POTTERIES

Staffordshire, in the northwest
of England, became the centre
of pottery manufacture. The
leading producer was Josiah
Wedgwood, who set up the
famous Etruria works in 1769.
He produced black and
cream-coloured wares, but his
most famous design was of an
unglazed blue decorated with
a raised white pattern.

*Wedgwood was inspired by
classical designs. He made a
copy of the Portland Vase, a fine
piece of Roman glassware.*

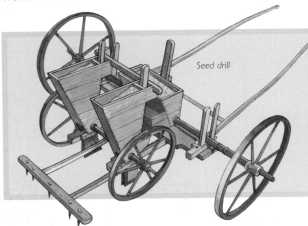

Seed drill

SCIENCE AND TURNIPS

Science and technology were beginning to
change farming as well as manufacture. In
1701 Jethro Tull invented a drill which
dropped seeds in rows instead of scattering
them across the field. In 1730 a retired
politician called Charles Townshed
(nicknamed 'Turnip') developed a new system
of improving the soil by switching ('rotating')
crops, using wheat, grass and turnips.

18

🙢 **1726**
Jonathan Swift publishes
Gulliver's Travels

🙢 **1728**
Irish Catholics no longer
allowed to vote

🙢 **1791**
Foundation of the United
Irishmen organization

🙢 **1793**
Relief Act restores vote to
Irish Catholics

🙢 **1795**
Foundation of the Orange
Order by Irish Protestants

IRISH REBELLION
AND UNION

I N THE 50 years after the Battle of the
Boyne, the Irish economy improved.
Trade passed along rivers, canals and much
improved roads to the the seaports of the east
and south. Farms prospered on the more fertile
lands, although the Irish–speaking peasant
farmers of the west struggled along on the
verge of famine. The Protestant ruling class
built splendid country homes. From the 1750s
onwards, Dublin was laid out with broad streets
of fine brick town houses and bridges over the
River Liffey. The population of Ireland rose to
about 5 million.

GULLIVER'S TRAVELS
Jonathan Swift was born in Dublin, of
English parents. He became known for
his poetry. He was appointed Dean of
St Patrick's Cathedral, in Dublin, and
campaigned against British restrictions
on Irish trade. In 1726 Swift wrote
Gulliver's Travels, in which the hero
describes his visits to various fantastic
worlds. The result is a bitter but
humorous look at the foolishness
of mankind.

🔻 *Swift uses the experiences of Gulliver
to point out human follies.*

DUBLIN AND LONDON
At the beginning of the 1700s,
Catholics made up 90 percent of the
Irish population, but owned only 14
percent of the land. The British
attitude to Ireland was that of a
colonial power. When Irish exports in
woollen cloth and cattle were so
successful that they threatened trade in
England, they were simply banned.
Catholics were not allowed to worship
freely or even to vote. Ireland still had
its own parliament in Dublin, but real
power lay in London.

◀ *The production of linen cloth from flax was
a major industry among the Protestants of
Ulster. Much of the work was home-based.*

WHO HOLDS POWER?

More and more people in Ireland, Protestant as well as Catholic, wanted to see political reform. One leader of opinion was a member of the Irish Parliament called Henry Grattan. Many of his supporters were inspired by the American War of Independence and the calls for freedom grew louder. When the French Revolution took place in 1789, the British decided it might be best if they went along with Grattan's demands.

UNITED IRISHMEN

After 1791 a Protestant from Kildare called Theobald Wolfe Tone recruited many Irish people to a society called the United Irishmen. It called for equal religious rights and Irish independence. At first it had support both from Protestant militias called the Volunteers and from Irish Catholics. It soon became linked with more radical groups and sought help from the revolutionary government in France. In 1796 a French revolutionary fleet appeared off Bantry Bay in the south, but was scattered by storms.

Politician Henry Grattan speaks to the Irish Parliament in 1780. He campaigned tirelessly for Ireland to be allowed to make its own laws.

DEFEAT OF THE REBELS

In May 1798 the Irish rebellion began in Wexford, and in August the French landed troops in support. It was too late. Both were defeated and many Irish rebels were hanged. Grattan's reforms were thrown out. A new Act of Union, in force from 1 January 1801, abolished the Irish parliament. A United Irishman called Robert Emmet attempted one more rising, in 1803. It failed and he too was hanged.

The 1798 rebellion came to an end at Vinegar Hill, near Wexford, on 21 June. That September, Wolfe Tone was captured. He committed suicide in prison.

20

≈ **1791**
Start of wars with revolutionary France

≈ **1798**
Battle of the Nile. Nelson defeats French off Egypt

≈ **1801**
Battle of Copenhagen. Nelson defeats Danish fleet.

≈ **1802**
Peace of Amiens closes French Revolutionary Wars

≈ **1803**
Start of Napoleonic Wars with France

THE NAPOLEONIC WARS

EORGE III's Britain and the revolutionary government in France were bitter enemies. They hated each other's politics and they were rivals for power. They went to war in 1791. Two remarkable characters made their name in the 11 years that followed. One was a popular British naval commander called Horatio Nelson. He defeated the French fleet at Aboukir Bay, Egypt, in 1798. The other was a brilliant French soldier called Napoleon Bonaparte. Napoleon had political ambitions.

Napoleon was a military genius, great law-maker and a ruthless politician.

A NEW EMPEROR IN EUROPE

A peace made between Britain and France in 1802 did not last. By 1804 the two countries were at war again – only by now Napoleon Bonaparte had crowned himself emperor of France and was planning to invade Britain. Round forts called 'Martello towers' were built to defend the Channel coast. The English anxiously peered through telescopes across the Straits of Dover. Mothers threatened naughty children that 'Boney' would come for them in the night if they did not behave – but the bogeyman did not invade.

The regiment of the Gordon Highlanders was raised in 1794 and was famed for its bravery. It took part in the ordeal of La Coruña, in the Peninsular War.

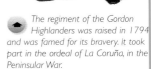

Napoleon's invasion of Russia was a step too far. His troops were defeated by the harsh winter conditions.

LAND AND SEA

In 1805 a French–Spanish fleet was defeated by Nelson off Cape Trafalgar, in Spain. Britain's navy ruled the seas. On land, however, Napoleon won stunning victories against the great powers of the day – Austria, Prussia, Russia. His empire soon stretched across Europe. In 1812 Napoleon invaded Russia, but his troops were caught in the winter snows and many perished. By 1814 France's enemies were in Paris. Napoleon was forced from power and exiled to the Mediterranean island of Elba.

The hugely popular admiral Horatio Nelson was killed in battle at Trafalgar, on the deck of HMS Victory.

1805
British defeat French and Spanish at Trafalgar. Nelson is killed

1806
Napoleon attempts blockade of Britain

1808
Peninsular War. British fight French in Spain

1814
End of war in Spain. Napoleon exiled to island of Elba.

1815
Napoleon escapes. Defeated by British and Prussians at Waterloo.

21

THE PENINSULAR WAR

In 1808 Napoleon invaded the Iberian peninsula (Portugal and Spain). He made his brother Joseph King of Spain. The British sent a force under Sir Arthur Wellesley (the later Duke of Wellington) to help Spanish and Portuguese resistance fighters. The British suffered setbacks during the campaign, with a desperate retreat to La Coruña in 1809. They won a great victory at Salamanca (1812) and also at Vittoria (1814).

The Duke of Wellington went into politics after Waterloo and became Prime Minister in 1828. He was opposed to the reform of Parliament.

WATERLOO

Napoleon slipped away from Elba and on 1 March 1815 he landed in France. Loyal troops rallied to him as he marched through the land. On 18 June they reached Waterloo, near Brussels, for a final and terrible battle. They were defeated by Prussian, Dutch and British troops under the command of the Duke of Wellington. The victors met in Vienna in 1815 to re-draw the map of Europe. Napoleon was sent to the remote Atlantic island of St Helena, where he died in 1821.

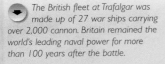

The British fleet at Trafalgar was made up of 27 war ships carrying over 2,000 cannon. Britain remained the world's leading naval power for more than 100 years after the battle.

BELOW DECKS

A sailor's life was tough during the 1700s and 1800s. Naval discipline was severe and punishment included floggings. Voyages were long, with hammocks slung between the decks for sleeping. Hard biscuits and salted-down meat were eaten, and a ration of rum was allowed. Battle conditions were terrifying, as cannon balls splintered masts and brought down rigging. In 1797 there were major mutinies by British sailors at Spithead and the Nore.

Press gangs were groups of sailors armed with cudgels. They roamed the ports, searching for new recruits. Young men were beaten up and forced to join the navy.

22

～ **1804**
World's first steam locomotive
built by Richard Trevithick

～ **1813**
Puffing Billy in use at Wylam
Colliery, Newcastle

～ **1819**
Paddle-steamer *Savannah*
arrives in Liverpool from USA

～ **1825**
Stephenson opens Stockton
to Darlington railway

～ **1829**
Stephenson's *Rocket* wins the
Rainhill trials

PUFFING BILLIES

THE COUNTRYSIDE of Britain and Ireland had been quiet and unspoiled throughout its history. In the 1800s, that peace was shattered. First came railway engineers, laying track, digging cuttings and building bridges. Then came clanking, steam-powered locomotives, huffing and puffing through the fields. Horses bolted in fright. Landowners cursed the infernal machines and sold their land to the railway companies to make a quick profit. The age of rail had arrived.

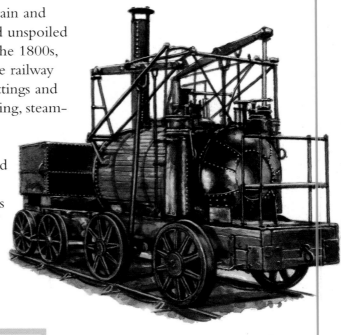

Puffing Billy, now in London's Science Museum, is the oldest steam locomotive still in existence.

THE RAINHILL TRIALS

In October 1829 the Manchester to Liverpool railway company offered a prize for the most reliable steam locomotive. Huge crowds gathered to see the locomotives battle it out on a length of track near Liverpool. *Perseverance* was much too slow. *Novelty* could travel at 30 mph (48 kph), but kept breaking down. *Sans Pareil* burned too much coal. The winner was the *Rocket*, built by George and Robert Stephenson.

The Stephensons' Rocket could average a speed of 15 mph (24 kph) and it did not break down once.

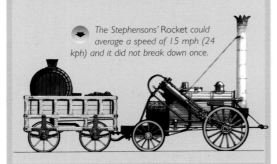

BIRTH OF THE RAILWAYS

The railway age began in 1804. A Cornish engineer called Richard Trevithick was working at Penydarren, near Merthyr Tydfil in South Wales. He mounted a steam engine on a wagon and created the world's first locomotive. He proved it could haul a heavy industrial load – and passengers too. By 1813 William Hedley's famous *Puffing Billy* was steaming away at Wylam Colliery, near Newcastle. Wylam was the birthplace of engineering genius George Stephenson. He greatly improved the design of locomotives and rails and between 1821 and 1825 he built the Stockton and Darlington Railway. His son Robert was also an engineer and in the 1840s and 50s he constructed magnificent railway bridges across the Menai Strait and the Conwy, Tyne and Tweed rivers.

∽∽ **1830**
Passenger service opens,
Liverpool to Manchester
railway

∽∽ **1833**
IK Brunel appointed chief
engineer of the Great
Western Railway

∽∽ **1837**
Euston Station opens, first
major London terminus

∽∽ **1843**
IK Brunel launches the iron
steamship *Great Britain*

∽∽ **1863**
World's first underground
railway opens in London

23

THE AGE OF STEAM

William Huskisson, Member of Parliament for
Liverpool, was run over and killed at the opening of
the Liverpool to Manchester passenger service in 1830.
However people were not put off. Rail travel gave
ordinary people freedom of movement. They could
travel to work in other towns. They could have holidays
by the sea. Industry was transformed too, as coal and
iron and products could be moved from one end of the
country to the other at ever higher speeds.

ISAMBARD KINGDOM BRUNEL

In 1879, the rail
bridge over the
River Tay in Scotland
collapsed during a storm.
A train fell into the waters
below, killing 75 people.
The scene is here
recreated with models.

ACROSS THE OCEAN

In 1819 an American paddle steamer docked in
Liverpool, and in 1821 the British steamer *Rising Star* left
Gravesend for South America. These early ships used sail
as well as steam, but by the 1830s steam-only crossings of
the Atlantic Ocean were also being made. The master of
building the new iron ships was the engineer IK Brunel.
Tall sailing ships were at this time reaching perfection in
their design, and it would be another 100 years before
they disappeared from the seas.

The son of an engineer, IK Brunel was
born in Portsmouth, England, in 1806.
He was a great builder of bridges,
tunnels and docks and in 1833 became
chief engineer of the Great Western
Railway. He also designed great
steamships for the Atlantic crossing.
Great Britain (1845) was driven by
propeller screws, and *Great Eastern*
(1858) held the record of the world's
biggest ever vessel for over 40 years.

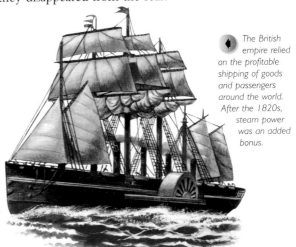

The British
empire relied
on the profitable
shipping of goods
and passengers
around the world.
After the 1820s,
steam power
was an added
bonus.

1834
Poor, elderly, orphans and disabled moved into 'workhouses'

1837
Population of United Kingdom is about 15 million

1842
It becomes illegal for women and children to work down mines

1848
Health of Towns Act, to improve water supply and drainage

1851
Over half the British population now lives in towns

THE FACTORY AGE

FAMILIES were leaving the countryside to seek work in the new factories and mines. They left a hard life for an even harder one. They toiled in the cotton mills of Manchester, in the steel mills of Sheffield, on the docksides of Liverpool, Glasgow and Newcastle-upon-Tyne. Industry depended on steam and steam depended on coal. The number of miners in Britain's coalfields doubled between 1851 and 1881.

Children worked underground in the mines, hauling coal waggons with chains or opening trap doors in the tunnels.

WORKING CONDITIONS

Many factory owners put profit above the health and safety of their workers. Children and young women were employed in wretched conditions in textile mills and mines. Small boys worked as sweeps, being made to crawl up tall, narrow chimneys in houses and factories until they bled. Furnaces were operated without proper safety checks. Workers in factories and mills were deafened by steam hammers and machinery. Hours were long and there were no holidays.

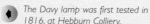

THE DAVY LAMP

Mining disasters killed hundreds of people in Victorian times. Deep underground, just one spark amongst the coal dust could set off an explosion, causing fires to rage or shafts to collapse. One invention which saved the lives of many miners was a safety lamp, developed by Cornish scientist Humphry Davy in 1815.

The Davy lamp was first tested in 1816, at Hebburn Colliery.

LAWS TO PROTECT WORKERS

Many Victorians were shocked by the conditions in which working people were now forced to live. In the 1840s and 50s, Lord Shaftesbury pushed new laws through Parliament which stopped women and children from working down the mines, and which limited the working day to 10 hours. Other laws followed in which factory conditions were brought under control. They were bitterly opposed by employers

THE GROWING CITIES

New cities were eating their way into the surrounding countryside. Terraces of red-brick houses sprawled back-to-back, as far as the eye could see. In big cities, families were packed into slums and children ran barefoot in the streets. There would be a pump in the yard and an outdoor toilet, both serving many families. Many toilets were still not flushed by water. Deadly diseases such as typhoid and cholera spread quickly in these unhealthy conditions. Gradually drainage was improved and new sewers were built under the cities.

SOOT AND SMOKE

In London, the Thames had become a foul-smelling, polluted river, deserted by its fish. In northern English cities the air was filled with smuts from factory chimneys. Buildings were covered in black soot. In winter, smoke and fog made it hard to find one's way. Gas lamps, which first appeared on streets during the Regency period, became common in the Victorian period.

VICTORIAN SCHOOLING

Children from poor homes received little education at all. 'Ragged schools' were set up to teach children from the factories and slums in the 1820s and 30s. From 1870 onwards, all children were sent to state-run primary schools for the first time. For the first time in the nation's history, poor people were receiving an education.

Smoking chimneys rise into the sky at Sheffield, centre of world steel production, in 1879. Drovers herded sheep and cattle from the countryside into cities. There they were slaughtered to feed the growing population.

26

1799
Socialist pioneer Robert Owen purchases New Lanark Mills, Scotland

1811
'Luddites' destroy industrial machinery in north of England

1819
Demonstrators killed in Manchester: the 'Peterloo' Massacre

1833
Slavery abolished in British empire

1834
'Tolpuddle Martyrs' – farm workers arrested for joining trade union

CHANGING SOCIETY

THE INDUSTRIAL age, which was now spreading rapidly through Europe and North America, completely changed society. However old methods of government stayed in place. Some people campaigned against injustice and tried to reform society. Many called for greater democracy. Some revolutionaries wanted the workers to seize power for themselves.

Prisoners are exercised in the yard. Political protest and petty crimes were met with harsh sentences. Many convicts were transported to prison colonies in Australia.

DICKENSIAN LONDON

Charles Dickens, born in 1812, had a hard childhood. His father was imprisoned for debt and he had to work in a factory making boot blacking. In 1828 he became a journalist and from the 1830s onwards began to write popular novels, many of them serialised in magazines. They tell us how the Victorians lived. *Oliver Twist* (finished in 1839) shows us life in the workhouse and the beggars and thieves of the London slums. Such tales shocked many people and encouraged social reform. Dickens died in 1870.

The poverty, violence, humour and humanity of Victorian London was recorded by Charles Dickens.

FIGHTERS AGAINST INJUSTICE

William Wilberforce, Member of Parliament for Hull, led a long campaign against the slave trade in the colonies. In 1807 British ships were banned from carrying slaves and in 1833, one month after Wilberforce died, slavery was finally abolished throughout the British empire.

Another great reformer was a Quaker called Elizabeth Fry, who from 1813 campaigned against terrible conditions in the prisons. Changes were made to the system, but Victorian prisons remained grim.

VIOLENT PROTEST

New machines meant fewer jobs. In 1811, laid-off Nottingham workers began to smash machinery. In the five years that followed, protests spread across northern England. The protestors claimed their leader was a 'General Ludd', so they were called 'Luddites'. Many were hanged or transported. New machines were replacing labourers on the farms, too. In 1830 farm workers in southern England destroyed threshing machines and set fire to haystacks. Their leader was commonly known as 'Captain Swing'.

| **1839** | **1844** | **1846** | **1877** | **1888** | 27 |
| First National Convention of the Chartist Movement | Cooperative movement set up in Rochdale for mutual help in trade and housing | Corn Laws, which kept the price of bread high, abolished by Robert Peel | Government takes central control of all prisons | Local Government Act – first County Council elections | |

A PEOPLE'S CHARTER

The Reform Act of 1832 gave the vote to more people and representation to the new cities. Between 1838 and 1848, working people campaigned for further reforms. They were called Chartists, because they presented a 'People's Charter' to Parliament. This demanded that all adult men should have the vote, that ballots should be secret and that anyone could become a Member of Parliament (MP). Parliament rejected the Charter, in 1840 and 1842. Mass protests and armed risings followed, but were put down by troops. However laws passed in 1867 and 1884 did bring in many democratic reforms.

 Trade unions campaigned for justice in the workplace. Sometimes members withdrew their labour, striking until their demands were met. Each union had its own embroidered banner.

TRADE UNIONS AND SOCIALISTS

Many working people organized trade unions, to fight for better conditions. Six Dorsetshire farm workers did this in 1834. Transported to Australia for this 'crime', they became known as the 'Tolpuddle Martyrs'. The richest people in Victorian society did not work. They used their money ('capital') to speculate, buying and selling shares. Socialists believed that the profits made by capitalists belonged rightfully to the workers who actually produced the goods.

THE COMMUNIST MANIFESTO

The writings of Marx (left) and Engels had a great influence on world history.

Karl Marx was a German writer on economics who moved to London. Friedrich Engels, another German, came to Manchester to work for his family's textile business. In 1848 Marx and Engels wrote the *Communist Manifesto*. They described how economic systems had developed through history and the conflict between social classes. They called upon workers all over the world to overthrow capitalism and create a society in which classes would exist no more.

In 1819, reformists meeting in St Peter's Fields, Manchester, were charged by mounted troops and volunteers. Eleven of the crowd were killed and 500 injured. Just 4 years after the Battle of Waterloo, the event became known as the Peterloo Massacre.

〜 **1796**
Edward Jenner pioneers
vaccination

〜 **1821**
Michael Faraday invents the
electric motor

〜 **1834**
Charles Babbage designs his
calculating machine

〜 **1841**
WH Fox Talbot pioneers
negative process for
photographs

〜 **1855**
Alfred Russel Wallace
publishes theories of evolution

ΠATURE, SCiEΠCE AΠD TECHΠOLOGY

T HE VICTORIANS were fascinated
by the natural world and how it
worked. There were breakthroughs
in the human understanding of physics,
chemistry, botany, zoology and geology.
Science was now studied at
universities, and introduced to the
public in splendid new museums,
botanical gardens and zoos.

LIFE ON EARTH

Many people were becoming interested in the
fossil remains of animals and plants. The scientists
Alfred Russel Wallace and Charles Darwin both travelled
the world, studying wildlife. They came to believe that
life forms on our planet had evolved, or gradually
developed, over many millions of years. Their ideas were
opposed by many Christians, who believed that the world
was only a few thousand years old and that all existing
creatures had been created by God in their present form.

*From 1831-1836 the crew of HMS
Beagle carried out a scientific survey
of South American waters. The chief scientist
on board was a young naturalist called
Charles Darwin. He collected and studied
fossils, animals and plants.*

INVENTIONS OF THE 1800s

Scientific discoveries were soon applied to
technology. New inventions in Western
Europe and North America transformed
industry, transport, medicine, commerce
and home life. Inventions in Great Britain
and Ireland included waterproofing of
cloth (Charles Macintosh,1832) and
cellulose (a form of plastic patented by
Alexander Parkes in 1855).

**calculating
machine**
*This mechanical calculator was
one of several designed by
Charles Babbage from the
1820s to 1840s. It may be
seen as an early attempt at
making a computer.*

bicycle power
*The first bicycle to be powered by pedals
was made by Scottish blacksmith Kirkpatrick
Macmillan in 1840. Pneumatic (air-filled) tyres
were first tried out in 1887 by John Boyd Dunlop.*

≈≈ **1856**
Henry Bessemer develops new method of making steel

≈≈ **1856**
William Perkin develops chemical dyes

≈≈ **1859**
Charles Darwin publishes *The Origin of Species*

≈≈ **1865**
Joseph Lister develops antiseptic medical treatments

≈≈ **1865**
Natural History Museum opens in Kensington, London

29

Joseph Lister's antiseptic spray was used in hospital wards and operating theatres from 1867 onwards.

MEDICAL RESEARCH

Great medical advances were made in Western Europe in the 1800s. An English doctor called Edward Jenner had carried out the first successful vaccination against smallpox in 1796. Vaccination against disease became widely accepted in Victorian hospitals, as did the antiseptic treatment of surgical instruments to kill germs. This change, brought in by the surgeon Joseph Lister in the 1860s, saved countless lives.

THE FOSSIL COLLECTOR

Mary Anning was born in Lyme Regis, Dorset in 1799. She was already a first-rate fossil collector as a child, discovering the first fossil skeleton of an *ichthyosaur* in 1810. In 1821 she found the first fossilized *plesiosaur* and in 1828 the first *pteranadon*.

By studying Mary Anning's fossil ichthyosaur, scientists could work out how such creatures lived in prehistoric times.

SCIENCE AND ELECTRICITY

Michael Faraday's discoveries about electricity and magnetism in the 1830s changed the way in which people lived. In 1878 Joseph Swan demonstrated an electric light bulb in Newcastle upon Tyne. The first electric telegraph was developed by WF Cooke and Charles Wheatstone in the 1830s. The telephone was first demonstrated in the USA in 1876, by Scottish-born inventor Alexander Graham Bell. The 'wireless telegraph' or radio was invented by the Italian scientist Guglielmo Marconi. He sent the first radio signal across the Atlantic Ocean, from Cornwall to Newfoundland, in 1901.

The Royal Botanical Gardens at Kew, to the west of London, became a world centre of research into plants and seeds. A fine palm house, built of glass and iron, was completed there in 1848.

30

≫≫ 1831
The Merthyr Rising – a workers' uprising in South Wales

≫≫ 1839
The Rebecca Riots in West Wales (until 1844)

≫≫ 1839
The Chartists march on Newport, in South Wales

≫≫ 1855
The first coal mine is opened in the Rhondda valley, South Wales

≫≫ 1858
The eisteddfod is revived as a yearly festival of music and poetry

VICTORIAN WALES

WALES HAD known peace since the Civil War, apart from a brief landing by French revolutionary troops at Fishguard in 1797. However the 1800s were less peaceful. There were no more wars or foreign invasions, but there was a period of violent social unrest brought about by rapid economic change.

LAND AND SEA

Most of Wales remained a land of small farms, where sheep grazed the green hillsides. In mid-Wales, the rivers were still fished from small wickerwork boats called coracles, as they had been since ancient times. Coastal dwellers caught herring and built ships and boats. In Victorian times, Welsh-built vessels sailed around the world. Among their cargoes was slate, shipped from the quarries of North Wales to roof the cities of the British empire. Another cargo was coal, exported through the growing port of Cardiff. For 130 years from 1855, coal would rule the economy of Wales.

REBECCA'S DAUGHTERS

A verse of the Bible says: '...they blessed Rebekah and said unto her, Let they seed (descendants) possess the gates of those which hate thee'. The poor people of West Wales knew all about gates – the hated toll gates where they had to pay taxes each time they transported goods along the highway. From 1839 onwards, groups of farmers attacked the gates and smashed them. Leaders of these protests took the name 'Rebecca' from the Bible.

The 'Rebecca' rioters jokingly disguised themselves as women, so that nobody would know their true identity. The riots lasted until 1844.

THE MERTHYR RISING

In 1829 there was widespread unemployment in South Wales and wages were cut. The troubles came to a climax in 1831. Prisoners were broken out of jail and a series of marches and riots turned into a full-scale uprising. In Merthyr Tydfil, troops were brought in to face a crowd of some 10,000 people. The soldiers opened fire, killing about 24 and wounding many more. A young miner called Richard Lewis, nicknamed 'Dic Penderyn' was later hanged for wounding a soldier, despite his innocence. The Merthyr rising was followed by ten years of bitter political protest.

Coal miners led a hard life. Many suffered from illnesses caused by the coal dust they breathed in underground.

1865
A Welsh colony is founded in Patagonia, South America

1872
University College of Wales opens at Aberystwyth

1886
The Young Wales movement (*Cymru Fydd*) is founded

1886
The 'Tithe War' – protests against tax paid to Church

1890
David Lloyd George becomes MP for Caernarfon

31

CHAPEL AND SCHOOLHOUSE

In the 1700s and 1800s, more and more Welsh people turned away from the Church of England to follow 'non-conformist' forms of worship. Chapels with names from the Bible, such as Bethesda or Jerusalem, now dotted the map of Wales. Whatever their beliefs, people still had to pay taxes, called tithes, to the Church of England. This led to many protests in the 1880s. It was the Chapels and their Sunday schools which helped to keep the Welsh language alive, for children were often punished for speaking their own language at the village school.

Cockle gatherers southwest Wales 1890s.

Spinning and knitting were the Welsh cottage industries. The 'national costume' was mostly a Victorian invention.

OLD AND NEW

The ancient poetry festivals called *eisteddfodau* were reinvented in the 1790s. After the 1850s, these annual meetings became a focus for Welsh cultural – and often political – life. Young Wales (*Cymru Fydd*), a movement for Welsh self-government, was started in 1886. It was soon eclipsed by support for a rising star in the world of politics, a young Liberal called David Lloyd George. He became MP for Caernarfon in 1890. By 1916 he would be Prime Minister.

WALES IN PATAGONIA

In 1865 a group of Welsh settlers sailed to Argentina, in South America. They founded a colony in the Chubut valley, in the remote region of Patagonia. Another colony was later founded at Cwm Hyfryd, at the foot of the Andes mountains.

The settlements prospered and the colonists built their own farms, chapels and law-courts. During the 1900s they became outnumbered by new Spanish and Italian settlers, but the Welsh language can still be heard in Patagonia to this day.

The Menai Suspension Bridge, an engineering marvel of its age, was built by Thomas Telford and opened in 1826. It lay on a new road built from London to Holyhead, the port for Ireland.

32

1820	1832	1843	1848	1850
Political protests end in harsh reprisals	The death of Sir Walter Scott, historical novelist	Disruption – Free Church breaks with Church of Scotland	Scotland linked with England by rail	The birth of Robert Louis Stevenson

VICTORIAN SCOTLAND

Q UEEN Victoria liked to visit Scotland. Her family would hunt the moors and fish for salmon. They made popular a romantic view of Scotland which was quite at odds with the harsh reality. In the Highlands, poor people were being forced from their cottages. In the industrial Lowlands, fortunes were being made while children starved in the sprawling slums of Glasgow.

The 'clearance' of the Highlands caused great hardship. In the 1830s and 40s things were made even worse by food shortages and starvation.

ROMANTIC TALES

In the1820s, readers across Europe were thrilled by the tales of adventure written by Sir Walter Scott. Many of his novels, such as *Rob Roy*, were rooted in exciting periods in Scottish history. Robert Louis Stevenson, who wrote from the 1870s to 90s, travelled far from his native Scotland. However he set several exciting tales such as *Kidnapped* in his homeland. He is remembered around the world for his story about the pirate Long John Silver, *Treasure Island*.

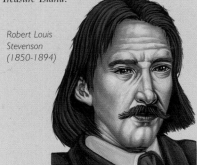

Robert Louis Stevenson (1850-1894)

HIGHLAND CLEARANCES

Between the 1750s and the 1860s, landowners in the Scottish Highlands reorganized their estates along more commercial lines. They brought in sheep, which were more profitable than cattle. In the Victorian age, they encouraged deer hunting and fishing. A large workforce was no longer needed and tenants simply stood in the way of the landowners' profits.

Families were evicted by force and their cottages were destroyed. By the 1860s the Highlands had become largely depopulated and the Gaelic language spoken there was under threat. It was the 1880s before the rights of remaining tenants were protected by law.

LEAVING THE OLD COUNTRY

Many of the evicted Highlanders sought work in the Lowland cities. Others gave up and sailed off to foreign lands. Many emigrated to the coastal regions and cities of eastern Canada, to the United States and Australia.

≈ **1850s**
Number of homeless people
in Scotland reaches 200,000

≈ **1884**
The Highland Land League is
founded

≈ **1886**
The Crofters' Act protects
the rights of Highland
tenants

≈ **1893**
Keir Hardie founds the
Independent Labour Party

≈ **1900**
Population of Glasgow
reaches 916,000

33

SCOTLAND AT WORK

The eastern ports of Scotland were home to large fleets of sailing ships, which trawled the North Sea for herring. Women worked on shore gutting and cleaning the fish. Textiles and iron were the major industries around Lanark and Glasgow, and the River Clyde became a great centre for shipbuilding and shipping. Dundee grew wealthy processing jute imported from the lands of the British empire. By the time of Queen Victoria's death in 1901, one in three Scots lived in the cities – in Edinburgh, Glasgow, Dundee or Aberdeen.

THE DISRUPTION

In 1843 there was a major crisis in the Church of Scotland. In this 'Disruption', large numbers of people left the established Church. They were unhappy with the way in which it was influenced by the state, so they set up their own Free Church. In an age when Churches were deeply involved in education and social welfare, this had a great effect on everyday life.

The tartan cloth of the Scottish Highlands, which had been banned after the Jacobite rebellion of 1745, was made fashionable once more by the novels of Sir Walter Scott and by the royal family.

RADICAL POLITICS

The economic changes in Scotland encouraged calls for political change. In the early 1800s a Welsh socialist called Robert Owen set up the New Lanark Mills, with the aim of benefiting the workers. In 1819–1820 there was widespread rioting and three Scottish radicals, James Wilson, Andrew Hardie and John Baird were hanged. Scotland remained a centre of Chartist and Liberal politics and in 1893 a former Scottish miner called Keir Hardie founded the Independent Labour Party, the forerunner of the modern Labour Party.

In the early days of the Industrial Revolution, few factory owners cared about working conditions. Robert Owen was an exception. The cotton mills he purchased from his father-in-law David Dale at New Lanark, in 1799, were designed to be healthy and clean. Owen provided workers with housing, a school and leisure activities.

34

∽ 1823
Daniel O'Connell founds the
Catholic Association

∽ 1829
Catholics receive voting rights
– 'Emancipation'

∽ 1842
The Young Ireland movement
is founded

∽ 1845
Famine after potato crop fails
(until 1848)

∽ 1858
Growth of the Irish
Republican Brotherhood

FAMINE IN IRELAND

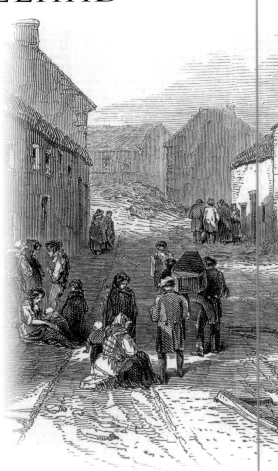

IN IRELAND, industry chiefly developed in the north. Belfast soon grew to be larger than the Irish capital, Dublin. Belfast's economy depended upon linen textiles, engineering and shipbuilding. At the same time, much of rural Ireland was suffering from poverty and hunger. Ireland may now have been part of the United Kingdom, but its citizens did not seem to be treated equally. The Union was challenged time after time.

O'CONNELL AND 'YOUNG IRELAND'

The fight for Irish Catholics to be able to vote was taken up by Daniel O'Connell, a popular lawyer known as 'the Liberator'. His campaign succeeded in 1829, but most Catholics did not own enough property to qualify for the vote. O'Connell went on to campaign against the Union with Great Britain. At first he was allied with a nationalist movement called 'Young Ireland', but its members soon disagreed with his policy of non-violence. They organized an armed uprising in 1848, but it was too small to succeed.

Daniel O'Connell, lawyer, politician and veteran campaigner for Irish rights, died in 1847, heartbroken by the tragedy of the famine.

THE IRISH FAMINE

The tenant farmers of rural Ireland lived a wretched life. The high rents they had to pay to landlords meant that they had to sell all the grain they could grow. For their own food, they relied on potatoes and little else. In 1845 the potato crop was struck by a blight, or mould. The people starved and began to die of fever and dysentery. The landlords never went hungry and crops that could have saved lives were exported to England. The blight continued and the famine lasted three years.

≈ **1875**
Charles Stuart Parnell is elected to Parliament

≈ **1879**
Michael Davitt founds Irish National Land League

≈ **1882**
The Phoenix Park murders, Dublin

≈ **1884**
The National League replaces the Land League

≈ **1886**
Home Rule Bill defeated in Parliament

35

LANDLORDS AND FENIANS

The famine left lasting bitterness. It was felt that the government had done very little to prevent the tragedy and that landlords had neglected their tenants. New campaigns were now launched to protect tenants, in a long 'land war'.

The Irish Republican Brotherhood grew up in the late 1850s. Its members, known as Fenians ('warriors') organized unsuccessful risings in 1865 and 1867 and campaigns of violence in England. Their aim was an independent Ireland.

In 1841 the population of Ireland was about 8 million. Perhaps 800,000 to a million of them died during the years of famine.

EMIGRATION

During the famine and the years that followed, some 1½ million Irish people left their homeland to seek a better life overseas. Many ended up in Glasgow, Liverpool or London. Others sailed to seek a new life in the United States, Canada and Australia. They left behind deserted villages – and large areas where the Irish language was no longer heard.

IRISH AMERICANS

Many Fenians did not live in Ireland, but in the large Irish communities that were growing up overseas. The Irish who had settled in the eastern United States kept the campaign for Irish independence alive.

Generation after generation left Ireland to search for work. Here crowds gather on the dockside. Conditions on the Atlantic crossing were often terrible, and in the days of the famine many people died during the voyage.

THE BOYCOTT

A new word entered the English language in 1880: 'to boycott'. It meant 'refusing to deal with someone'. The name came from Charles Boycott, the land agent for Lord Erne, who had an estate in County Mayo. When Boycott would not lower the rents, the tenants protested by refusing to speak or deal with him in any way.

HOME RULE FOR IRELAND?

In the 1870s the campaign for Irish tenants' rights was taken up by a Protestant politician called Charles Stewart Parnell. He won the support of many Fenians, but was cleared of involvement in acts of terror such as the murder of two English officials in Phoenix Park, Dublin, in 1882. Parnell's constant demands for 'home rule' by an Irish parliament were at last supported in London by the Liberal leader, William Gladstone. New laws were brought in to protect tenant's rights in the 1880s, but when Parnell died in 1891, Parliament still had not agreed to Irish home rule.

36

∽∽ **1853**
Russia occupies Moldavia and Wallachia (Romania)

∽∽ **1854**
March: British and French enter Crimean War

∽∽ **1854**
20 September: Battle of the River Alma

∽∽ **1854**
25 October: Battle of Balaclava, Charge of the Light Brigade

∽∽ **1854**
5 November: Battle of Inkerman, heavy casualties

THE GREAT POWERS

RUSSIA HAD grown into a huge empire, stretching from Central Europe into Asia. In 1853 it invaded the region now known as Romania. At that time, this was ruled by the powerful Ottoman empire of the Turks. Turkey went to war with Russia. Because the United Kingdom and France wanted to stop Russia gaining control of the Balkan region, they joined forces with the Turks.

THE CRIMEAN WAR

In 1854 France and Britain sent troops to the Black Sea, even though the Austrians had already forced the Russians out of Romania. The allies landed on the Crimean peninsula, part of the Russian empire, and laid siege to the Russian naval base of Sebastopol. They won victories on the River Alma, at Balaclava and Inkerman, but the war is chiefly remembered for a disastrous charge by the British cavalry. Ordered in error to launch a direct attack on Russian guns at Balaclava, the Light Brigade galloped to certain death. The war was won in 1855, when a French force finally burst through the defences of Sebastopol.

The charge of the 600-strong Light Brigade at Balaclava in 1854 was commemorated by the great Victorian poet Alfred, Lord Tennyson. He described them riding 'Into the jaws of Death, Into the mouth of Hell'.

1855
astopol falls to the British French

1856
Treaty of Paris ends the Crimean War

1856
Florence Nightingale starts the training of nurses

1856
Journalist WH Russell publishes his Crimean War despatches

1878
Congress of Berlin settles Russian and Turkish borders

THE LADY WITH THE LAMP

The blunder at Balaclava showed that the British army was run by ageing aristocrats who had little understanding of modern warfare. The troops were poorly dressed and equipped and died in their thousands from cholera and frostbite. One person did care for the wounded and dying. In 1854 an English woman called Florence Nightingale arrived at Scutari (Üsküdar) with 38 nurses. With her strict concern for hygiene, she saved countless lives. On return to England, Florence Nightingale started the training of professional nurses.

PRIME MINISTERS OF THE UNITED KINGDOM

✤ Benjamin Disraeli (Conservative)	1860
✤ William Gladstone (Liberal)	1868–1874
✤ Benjamin Disraeli (Conservative)	1874–1880
✤ William Gladstone (Liberal)	1880–1885
✤ Marquess of Salisbury (Conservative)	1885–1886
✤ William Gladstone (Liberal)	1886
✤ Marquess of Salisbury (Conservative)	1886–1892
✤ William Gladstone (Liberal)	1892–1894
✤ Earl of Rosebery (Liberal)	1894–1895
✤ Marquess of Salisbury (Conservative)	1895–1902

Florence Nightingale visited the sick and wounded by night, with a lantern. She became known as the 'lady with the lamp'.

REPORTS FROM THE BATTLEFIELD

Magazines such as the *Illustrated London News*, with its drawings of current events, were very popular with the Victorians. However reports of the Crimean War, published by *The Times* newspaper, shocked the public. They were sent directly from the war zone by an Irish journalist called William Howard Russell. It was during the Crimean War that the first war photographs were taken, too. For the first time in history people could read about distant battles and see the reality of warfare for themselves.

This van was used to process photographs taken during the Crimean War.

RIVAL NATIONS AND EMPIRES

New nation states were being founded across Europe. Italy united as a single kingdom in 1861. In 1867 the twin nation of Austria–Hungary was created. In 1871 Germany became a single country, for the first time. Its *Kaiser* (emperor) was Wilhelm I. He was followed onto the throne in 1888 by Wilhelm II, a grandson of Queen Victoria. This was an age of petty nationalism, or 'jingoism', in which each nation tried to outdo the others. By 1914, this would lead to the bloodiest war in history. In the meantime, European nations were building up vast empires overseas. The British empire now

jEWELS iN THE CROWN

B Y 1869, ships could sail directly to Asia through the new Suez Canal. Passengers included troops and merchants, who were rapidly turning Asia's ancient empires into colonies from which they could reap rich rewards. Britain's Asian empire grew to take in the countries and ports now known as Aden, Pakistan, India, Bangladesh, Sri Lanka, Myanmar (Burma), Malaysia, Singapore, Brunei and Hong Kong.

BRITISH INDIA

British rule had a great influence on India, and India impressed the empire-builders in return. Generations of them came to know India's hot, dusty plains better than the distant islands of 'home'. They fought the Afghans along the Northwest Frontier, built railways, planted tea or played polo. Many of them were racists, who believed themselves to be superior to the Indians. Others worked hard for the country and its people, but British rule did not bring an end to poverty or starvation.

Indian brokers examine bales of cotton in Bombay. British cotton mills obtained about 20 percent of their cotton from India. However this changed when the civil war in the United States (1861-65) interrupted supplies from America. The result was a boom in Indian cotton.

THE JUNGLE BOOKS

Rudyard Kipling was an English writer born at Bombay, India in 1865. He was fascinated by India and wrote short stories and poems about common soldiers, officers and Indian life. For children he wrote the two classic *Jungle Books*. Although Kipling was inspired by the empire, he often criticized imperialism and realised that it must pass.

THE INDIAN MUTINY

In 1857 Indian soldiers (or 'sepoys') serving Britain's East India Company rose up against their commanders in northern India. In some regions this mutiny turned into a general uprising. The rebels captured Delhi and laid siege to Kanpur and Lucknow. They were defeated in 1858. From now on, however, India would be ruled not by the Company but by the British government itself. In

⚏ **1842**
Britain gains South China port of Hong Kong as colony.

⚏ **1857**
The Indian Mutiny against the East India Company

⚏ **1858**
British government takes over the rule of India

⚏ **1860**
British and French troops sack Beijing, China

⚏ **1877**
Victoria is created Empress of India

39

THE CHINA TRADE

One crop grown in India was the opium poppy. It was made into a very addictive drug. Britain exported Indian opium to China. When the Chinese government tried to ban this deadly trade in 1839, Britain declared war. Britain won this shameful conflict and as a result gained the Chinese port of Hong Kong as a colony. The rest of China remained an independent empire, but was forced to grant more and more trading rights to Western nations. British and French troops sacked Beijing, the Chinese capital, in 1860.

IN SOUTHEAST ASIA

The British, French and Dutch all sought to control the rich Southeast Asian trade in spices, rubber, timber and minerals. An Englishman called Stamford Raffles founded Singapore in 1819, and in 1826 it joined Penang and Malacca as the Straits Settlements. In 1841 another Englishman, James Brooke, helped to defeat a rebellion against the Sultan of Brunei, on the island of Borneo. As a reward he was made the ruler, or Rajah, of Sarawak.

One of China's chief exports was tea. Fast merchant ships called clippers raced back to Britain with their cargo. Clippers were the finest sailing vessels ever built. One of them, the Cutty Sark, can still be seen beside the River Thames at Greenwich, London.

During the Indian Mutiny, the city of Delhi was held by the rebels for three months. British troops under the command of Sir Colin Campbell stormed its defences in September 1857.

40

〜 **1793**
Settlement of the first free colonists in Australia

〜 **1840**
Treaty of Waitangi: Britain claims New Zealand

〜 **1845**
Start of First Maori War, New Zealand (Second War 1860)

〜 **1851**
Start of the gold rush in Australia

〜 **1854**
Miners' revolt at Eureka, near Ballarat, Australia

TO THE ENDS
OF THE EARTH

BRITAIN'S EMPIRE grew to take in the vast, unknown land of Australia, as well as New Zealand and many South Pacific islands. At first, the British only used as Australia as a place to send prisoners. Many convicts died on the outward voyage and life in the prison colonies was harsh. Some escaped and took ship to New Zealand.

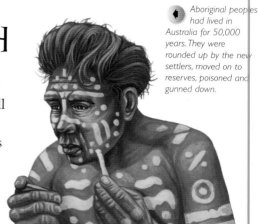

Aboriginal peoples had lived in Australia for 50,000 years. They were rounded up by the new settlers, moved on to reserves, poisoned and gunned down.

The discovery of gold in Australia led to further exploration and a rapid increase in the settler population, which reached a million in 1861.

BRITAIN'S AUSTRALIAN COLONIES

By 1793 the first free settlers had arrived in New South Wales, but it was 1868 before all transportation of convicts to Australia came to an end. Settlers gradually opened up the dry lands of the interior. New or breakaway colonies were founded – Van Diemen's Land (Tasmania) in 1804, Western Australia in 1829, South Australia in 1836, Victoria in 1851, Queensland in 1859. By 1861 an expedition led by Robert O'Hara Burke and William Wills had made the hazardous journey from Melbourne to the north coast.

GOLD NUGGETS, WOOLLY SHEEP

In 1851 gold was discovered in New South Wales. Settlers poured into Australia in search of a fortune. The miners, or 'diggers', had few legal rights and a major revolt took place at Eureka, near Ballarat in Victoria, in 1854. Thirty miners were killed by mounted police. Another great source of wealth was sheep farming. By 1890 there were 100 million sheep in Australia.

⚙ **1861**
Burke and Wills cross the interior of Australia

⚙ **1868**
Last transportation of convicts to Australia

⚙ **1874**
Fiji becomes part of the British empire

⚙ **1901**
Australian colonies unite as a federal Commonwealth

⚙ **1907**
New Zealand becomes a Dominion of the British empire

41

WHOSE AUSTRALIA?

Between the 1823 and 1855 the Australian colonists gained increasing rights to govern their own affairs, and by 1901 the various colonies had come together to form a federation, the Commonwealth of Australia. There was a new Parliament – but the true Australians, the Aborigines, were denied the vote until 1967.

NED KELLY THE OUTLAW

Ned Kelly, the son of an Irish convict, was born in Victoria in 1855. He became an outlaw, or 'bushranger', whose gang robbed banks and stole cattle. After a train was held up at Glenrowan, three of the gang were killed. Ned Kelly was captured and hanged in1880.

When Ned Kelly was finally captured he was dressed in home-made armour.

NEW ZEALAND AND THE MAORIS

New Zealand was inhabited by the Maoris, a Polynesian people, and by a small number of mostly British settlers. In 1840 the British signed a treaty with Maori chiefs at Waitangi and New Zealand became a British colony. The settlers failed to honour the treaty and Maoris fought them from 1845 to 1847 and again from 1860 to 1872. From 1856, the settlers had their own Parliament. Many gold miners and farmers now arrived in New Zealand. From the 1880s, advances in refrigeration meant that lamb could be shipped back to Britain.

ACROSS THE PACIFIC

European seafarers, planters and Christian missionaries were now spreading out through the islands of the South Pacific. Many islanders fell victim to kidnappers called 'blackbirders', and were shipped off illegally to forced labour in Australia. Fiji became British in 1874 and Britain claimed southeastern New Guinea (Papua) in 1884. By the end of the century, most Pacific islands were under foreign rule.

This war canoe was made by Solomon Islanders. Britain gained control of these Pacific islands between 1893 and 1900.

42

捣 **1806**
Cape Colony, South Africa,
under British rule

捣 **1873**
Ashanti Wars on the Gold
Coast (Ghana) – to 1901

捣 **1873**
David Livingstone dies in what
is now Zambia

捣 **1878**
The Zulu War in South Africa
(to 1879)

捣 **1881**
First South African ('Boer')
War

INTO AFRICA

T HE BRITISH may have ended their part in the slave trade, but it remained a curse in many parts of Africa. European explorers and Christian missionaries were now braving lions, spears and tropical fevers as they led expeditions into the interior. They were followed by traders, prospectors, colonists. big-game hunters – and soldiers. By the end of Queen Victoria's reign, almost all of Africa was under European rule.

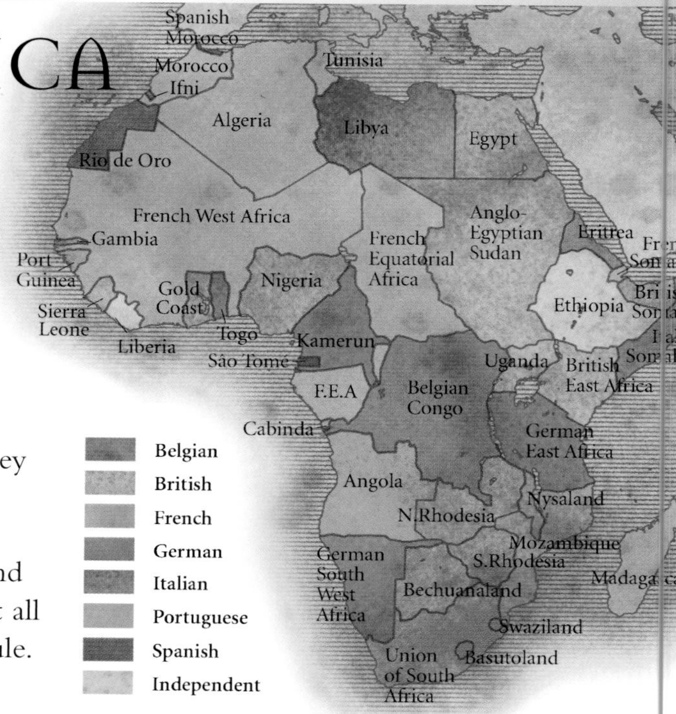

Map labels: Spanish Morocco, Morocco, Ifni, Tunisia, Algeria, Libya, Egypt, Rio de Oro, French West Africa, Anglo-Egyptian Sudan, Eritrea, French Somaliland, Gambia, French Equatorial Africa, British Somaliland, Port Guinea, Gold Coast, Nigeria, Kamerun, Ethiopia, Italian Somaliland, Sierra Leone, Liberia, Togo, São Tomé, Uganda, British East Africa, F.E.A., Belgian Congo, Cabinda, German East Africa, Angola, Nysaland, N.Rhodesia, Mozambique, German South West Africa, S.Rhodesia, Madagascar, Bechuanaland, Swaziland, Union of South Africa, Basutoland

Legend:
- Belgian
- British
- French
- German
- Italian
- Portuguese
- Spanish
- Independent

The European powers competed with each other to control Africa. There were wars of resistance by peoples all over Africa, but they were helpless against troops armed with modern firearms. This map shows who ruled Africa in 1890.

SHARING THE SPOILS

Africans were now used as a labour force, but were often little better off than slaves. Their job was to extract the riches of the continent for their colonial rulers. In southern and eastern Africa the best farmland was seized by white settlers. At the Conference of Berlin in 1884–1885, whole regions of Africa were shared out between rival European powers. They knew almost nothing about the peoples living there and cared little for their needs.

EAST AFRICAN LANDS

In 1887 the British East African Company leased the Kenya coast from its ruler, the Sultan of Zanzibar. Eight years later, Britain claimed the interior, eventually creating a colony called Kenya. British rule extended into neighbouring Uganda and (after 1918) into Tanganyika (now the mainland of Tanzania). Railways were built by labourers brought in from India, while farmers seized the highlands and planted coffee.

Explorers and traders led armed expeditions into the interior from the East African coast. They hired porters to carry their equipment.

DAVID LIVINGSTONE

When the Scottish explorer David Livingstone died of fever in what is now Zambia, in 1873, his African servants preserved his body and carried it all the way to the coast, a journey on foot which took them nine months. Livingstone was a Christian missionary and a tireless campaigner against slavery, who explored the lands around the River Zambezi.

Livingstone was the first European to see the Victoria Falls and Lake Nyasa.

SUEZ TO SUDAN

In 1875 Britain became chief shareholder in the new, French-built Suez Canal, which cut through Egypt. Britain soon became more powerful in Egypt than the government itself. It also took control of Sudan, to the south. In 1877 British General Charles Gordon became governor of Sudan. He was killed at Khartoum in 1885, after an uprising led by the fiery religious leader Muhammad Ahmed, known as the *Mahdi* ('saviour'). In 1898 the British avenged Gordon's death at Omdurman, killing 11,000 Sudanese warriors.

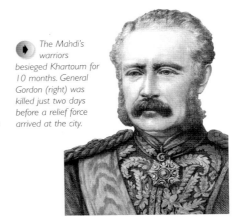

The Mahdi's warriors besieged Khartoum for 10 months. General Gordon (right) was killed just two days before a relief force arrived at the city.

ASHANTI GOLD

West Africa's Guinea Coast was also occupied by British empire builders. In 1874 they invaded Ashanti territory and destroyed the capital, Kumasi. In 1901 these lands became Gold Coast colony (modern Ghana), with an economy based on cocoa. Between 1861 and 1906 the huge colony of Nigeria was also created, out of various West African territories and trading posts.

This splendid leather helmet, decorated with gold and silver, was worn at the Ashanti royal court.

SOUTHERN AFRICA

In 1806 the British gained control of Cape Colony, South Africa. The Dutch had settled the area since the 1650s and resented British rule. In 1837 these 'Afrikaners' or 'Boers' ('farmers') left the Cape. They headed for the interior, where they founded independent republics. When rich reserves of diamonds and gold were discovered there, British empire builder and businessman Cecil Rhodes saw this as a great opportunity. His miners poured in the area, but Afrikaner president, Paul Kruger would not give these outsiders rights in his farmers' republic. In 1899 a bitter war broke out between the British and the Boers. Peace was made in 1902 and the Union of South Africa was formed in 1910.

In South Africa, the British clashed with highly disciplined armies of the Zulu nation. These inflicted a crushing defeat on British troops at Isandhlwana in 1879. Away from the main battlefield, a small British force at Rorke's Drift (right) fought off attacks by about 4,000 Zulus. British rule soon spread out from South Africa into the countries we now call Lesotho, Botswana, Swaziland, Malawi, Zambia and Zimbabwe.

44

<svg>~~</svg> **1831**
British Guiana (Guyana)
becomes a colony

<svg>~~</svg> **1833**
Falkland Islands (*Islas Malvinas*)
become a British colony

<svg>~~</svg> **1834**
Slavery ends in Britain's
Caribbean islands (to 1838)

<svg>~~</svg> **1840**
Act of Union between Lower
and Upper Canada

<svg>~~</svg> **1862**
British Honduras (Belize)
becomes British colony

NORTH AND SOUTH ATLANTIC

The Inuit or Eskimo people lived in scattered settlements in the Canadian Arctic.

Q UEEN Victoria's empire took in remote Atlantic outposts such as St Helena, Tristan da Cunha and the Falkland Islands. It governed Bermuda and many Caribbean islands. On the American mainland, the lands now known as Guyana and Belize were all part of her empire, as well as Canada's vast forests and prairies.

CANADA BECOMES A DOMINION

In 1791 Canada had been divided along the Ottawa River. Lower Canada was the French-speaking area, while Upper Canada was English-speaking. These two were united in 1840, taking in the provinces of Ontario, Quebec, Nova Scotia and New Brunswick. A parliament was set up in 1849 and in 1858 Ottawa became the Canadian capital, the personal choice of Queen Victoria. In 1867 Canada was made a self-governing Dominion of the British empire. This was set up along federal lines, with each province keeping its own elected assembly.

PRAIRIES AND FORESTS

Canada continued to expand into lands occupied by its First Peoples and by the Métis. They rose up in rebellion in 1867, under the leadership of Louis Riel, but were defeated. Manitoba joined Canada (1870), British Columbia (1871), Prince Edward Island (1873), Alberta and Saskatchewan (1905). Poor farmers from all over Europe arrived to settle the Canadian prairies, and prospectors searching for gold arrived in the remote Northwest in 1896. Canada prospered from its timber, oil, mineral wealth and fisheries. The last province to join the Canadian federation was Newfoundland, in 1949.

The building of railways encouraged settlement of Canada's prairie provinces and the far west. The Canadian Pacific Railway spanned the country coast-to-coast by 1885.

1867
Canada becomes a Dominion of the British empire

1867
Canadian *Métis* rise under Louis Riel

1880
Rights of Canada's First Peoples limited by new Indian Act

1885
The Canadian Pacific Railway is opened

1896
Goldrush in the Canadian Klondike region

45

THE CARIBBEAN ISLANDS

In the 1830s, slavery was ended in Britain's Caribbean colonies, which were known as the 'West Indies'. Many freed slaves moved off the plantations and lived by farming small plots of land, or fishing. They remained desperately poor and there was an uprising against the British governor on Jamaica in 1865, led by George William Gordon and Paul Bogle. On Trinidad, contracted labourers were brought in from Asia to work on the sugar plantations, but the majority population throughout the Caribbean region was now of African descent.

CARIBBEAN CARNIVAL

Trinidad and some other Caribbean islands began to celebrate Carnival in the 1800s. This festival had been brought to the region from Catholic Europe. At first, slaves were not allowed to take part, but after they were freed they made it their own, with dancing, singing and drumming to African rhythms. From the Asian community came spectacular costumes and masks.

 Carnival originally marked the beginning of Lent, the Christian period of fasting.

Slavery had dominated the culture and economy of the Caribbean for 300 years, when it was finally phased out in the 1830s.

IN CENTRAL AND SOUTH AMERICA

In 1862 a small region of the Central American coast, occupied by British loggers, was made into a colony called British Honduras (modern Belize). In South America, sugar-producing British Guiana (modern Guyana) had become a colony in 1834. British people played an important part in the development of other South American lands, too, building railways high into the Andes mountains.

Weathered wood, verandahs, shutters and porches are a reminder of the colonial age in Belize, formerly British Honduras.

İNDEX

Look up subjects to be found in this book.
Illustrations are shown in *italic* print.

ACKNOWLEDGEMENTS

**The publishers would like to thank the following
sources for the use of their images:**

Page 10 (B/L) McMaster University Library, Ontario; 13 (T/R)
Bettmann/Corbis; 14 (B/L) Bob Krist/Corbis; 18 (R/C)
Bettmann/Corbis; 19 (T/R) Corbis, (B/L) Mary Evans Picture
Library; 21 (R/C) Bridgeman Art Library, (B) Archivo
Iconografico/Corbis; 24 (R/C) Mary Evans Picture Library;
27 (T/R) Bridgeman Art Library, (L/C) Topham Picturepoint,
(B/R) Mary Evans Picture Library; 29 (B) Camera Press;
30 (T/R) Mary Evans Picture Library, (B/R) Topham
Picturepoint; 31 (T/R) & (L/C) Topham Picturepoint;
33 (B/R) Eileen Tweedy/The Art Archive; 35 (C/R) Topham
Picturepoint; 37 (B/L) Mary Evans Picture Library;
40 (B/L) Topham Picturepoint; 43 (C/L) Museum of
Mankind/Bridgeman Art Library; 45 (B/L)
Barnabas Bosshart/Corbis
All other photographs from MKP Archives

**The publishers would like to thank the artists whose
work appears in this book:**

Richard Berridge/SpecsArt, Peter Dennis/Linda Rogers
Associates, Nicholas Forder, Terry Gabbey/AFA,
Richard Hook/Linden Artists, Andy Lloyd Jones/Allied Artists,
Janos Marffy, Terry Riley, Pete Roberts/Allied Artists,
Martin Sanders, Rob Sheffield, Rudi Vizi,
Mike White/Temple Rogers